Dear Parent:
Your child's love of reading starts here!

Every child learns to read in a different way and at his or her own speed. Some go back and forth between reading levels and read favorite books again and again. Others read through each level in order. You can help your young reader improve and become more confident by encouraging his or her own interests and abilities. From books your child reads with you to the first books he or she reads alone, there are I Can Read Books for every stage of reading:

SHARED READING
Basic language, word repetition, and whimsical illustrations, ideal for sharing with your emergent reader

BEGINNING READING
Short sentences, familiar words, and simple concepts for children eager to read on their own

READING WITH HELP
Engaging stories, longer sentences, and language play for developing readers

READING ALONE
Complex plots, challenging vocabulary, and high-interest topics for the independent reader

ADVANCED READING
Short paragraphs, chapters, and exciting themes for the perfect bridge to chapter books

I Can Read Books have introduced children to the joy of reading since 1957. Featuring award-winning authors and illustrators and a fabulous cast of beloved characters, I Can Read Books set the standard for beginning readers.

A lifetime of discovery begins with the magical words **"I Can Read!"**

Visit www.icanread.com for information
on enriching your child's reading experience.

Pinkalicious®
and the Pirates

To Max
—V.K.

The author gratefully acknowledges
the artistic and editorial contributions of
Daniel Griffo and Jacqueline Resnick.

I Can Read Book® is a trademark of HarperCollins Publishers.

Pinkalicious and the Pirates
Copyright © 2018 by Victoria Kann

PINKALICIOUS and all related logos and characters are trademarks of Victoria Kann. Used with permission.

Library of Congress Control Number: 2017954079

ISBN 978-0-06-256699-7 (trade bdg.) — ISBN 978-0-06-256698-0 (pbk.)

22 CWM 10 9 8
❖
First Edition

I Can Read!

BEGINNING
1
READING

Pinkalicious®
and the Pirates

by Victoria Kann

HARPER

An Imprint of HarperCollinsPublishers

On Saturday morning,

a seagull landed on my windowsill.

It had a note in its beak.

The note was from my friend Aqua.

Aqua is a merminnie.

A merminnie is a miniature mermaid!

That afternoon,

Peter and I went to the cove.

We brought our beach toys,

because Aqua loves to play.

"Aqua? Aqua?" I called.

I didn't see Aqua anywhere.

"Wow, look at that!" said Peter.

He pointed to a ship in the cove.

There were two men on deck.

"They don't look like regular sailors,"
I said.

"That's because it's a pirate ship!"
Peter said.

The pirates were yelling.

"Argh! Mine are better!"

yelled one.

"Yarrr! Mine are MUCH better!"

yelled the other.

"I'm scared," Peter said.

I shivered.

I was also scared.

Suddenly, I heard a noise.

"EEEE!"

It was a scream,

and it was coming from the ship!

"That sounds like Aqua!" I said.
"She must have been captured
by the evil pirates."
"Yikes!" said Peter.
"I hope they don't make her
walk the plank."

I knew I had to be brave.

"Aqua won't walk the plank," I said,

"because we're going to save her."

Peter went pale.

"What about the pirates?" he asked.

I looked at my kite.

It gave me an idea.

I shared my plan with Peter.

I tried to fly my kite,

but the wind was very strong!

"Help me!" I said to Peter.

He held the kite string with me.

Together, we ran toward the ship.

Suddenly, the kite
was swept up by the wind.
"Kites ahoy!" I said.
My kite flew into the pirates
and tangled them all up,
just as I had planned.

"Argh!" yelled the pirates.

"We're stuck!"

Peter and I waded through the water
and sneaked up the ship's ladder.

Peter put his buckets over

the pirates' heads.

"Blimey, I can't see!"

said the captain.

"Quick, we have to find Aqua,"

I said to Peter.

We looked everywhere for Aqua,

but all we saw was a parrot.

The parrot landed on my shoulder.

"CookiEEEE!" it screamed.

"CookiEEEE!"

My eyes widened.

It was the scream we'd heard before!

Peter glared at me.

"That is not Aqua," he said.

"Oh dear," I said.

"Heave ho, let us go!"
the pirates yelled.

"What do we do?" Peter squeaked.

Suddenly, I heard a familiar voice.

"Ahoy, Pinkalicious!"

It was Aqua!

"Sorry I'm late.

I've been looking for you two,"

Aqua called up from the ocean.

"Did you meet my friend

Captain Pinkbeard?"

"Your friend?" I repeated.

"Uh-oh . . ."

"Blimey!" said Peter.

Quickly, we set the pirates free.

"We're good pirates," they told us.

"Then why were you yelling before?"
I asked Captain Pinkbeard.

"The first mate and I were
having a disagreement," he said.

The captain opened a treasure chest.

A yummy smell came out of it.

The chest was filled with cookies!

"The pirates bake the best treats

on the high seas," said Aqua.

"What was your disagreement about?"
I asked.

"I think our new cookies should have
pink sprinkles," said the captain.

"Well I like purple sprinkles,"
said the first mate.

"Yarrrr in luck," said Peter.

"Pinkalicious is a cookie expert."

We went down to the galley

where the pirates made cookies.

I decorated the cookies

with pink and purple sprinkles.

"You can never have
too many sprinkles," I said.
The pirates tasted my cookies.
"That's true!" said Captain
Pinkbeard.

"Cookies for everyone!"
said Captain Pinkbeard.
"Now your cookies are perfect
just the way they ARGH!" I said.